Call It Genocide

(Biafra's Quest for Freedom and the Price of Silence)

A Play By

Eric Martin

October 2024

DEDICATION. I wrote this play for Biafra and its Christian people, who were subjected to a genocidal military campaign between 1967 and 1970. Over half a million innocent civilians were killed by numerically superior and better armed Nigerian Muslim forces. The betrayal of the Biafran people by the Western powers and the support the Soviet Union gave to the Muslim forces caused the collapse of the Biafran resistance. When the last strongholds fell in 1970, thousands of Biafran soldiers were executed, and the Christian population was ravaged. Biafra was wiped out militarily, but the spirit of freedom never died and is growing ever stronger. Biafra will live again, and the crime of genocide will not simply go away. There will be justice, and there will be accountability...not just for the commanders of the Muslim forces, but for the western and Soviet leaders who encouraged the slaughter. I will never forget the sacrifice the Biafran people made for their freedom for their right to live as Christians.

I also dedicate this play to my Biafran friends: Tony Okafor, Joel Chima, John Okongwu, and Frank Ihekwaba. They helped me and the Reverend James Dunn establish the Edinburgh University Biafran Student Appeal in 1968. I will never forget their courage and determination to defy the ruling global powers who abandoned Christians to savagery.

Characters

TONY NWOKEDI: He is the diplomatic representative of Benugu, a Christian enclave under siege by Islamic armies. He is 35, a distinguished graduate of Oxford University, an Anglophile, and a devoted Christian. He heads the Benugu Office, the unofficial embassy of his nation in Britain. In his speech and manner, he is an English gentleman.

SIR HUGH WINTHROP: Sir Hugh is the Foreign Secretary, a devoted socialist, and stalwart of the Lab our Party. He is of working-class origins and has overcome the obstacles of the class system in Britain. He is around 60 years of age, a man of integrity who is committed to the ideal of a fair and just society. He is old-fashioned in his honesty, unwilling to compromise his humanist values.

JAMES DONALD: He is 45, the Assistant or Under-Secretary of Sir Hugh Winthrop. A highly educated and polished professional diplomat. He embodies the traditional values and principles which once made Britain respected amongst civilized peoples. He is unwavering in his commitment to the truth and to human rights.

THE PRIME MINISTER, HAROLD CROSSMAN: He is around 60, an imposing man physically, from a working-class background in the North of England. He is a career opportunist and ruthless in attaining his political ambitions. Capable of a refined dissimulation, he navigates his way through the defenses of his opponents. He does not have any non- negotiable moral principles but is guided by self-interest.

GENERAL MUSA, THE AMBASSADOR OF THE STATE OF BENGARA. General bin Musa is a hardened soldier who delighted in killing, raping, and torturing his enemies. He boasts of his atrocities and is dismissive of all criticism. He is an Islamist who believes that Islam must rule the world and force all non-Muslims to convert to his religion. He and his fellow Islamists in the ruling junta of Bengara are committed to wiping out the Christian rebel state of Benugu. He is around 60, obese, and ugly.

THE ARCHBISHOP OF CANTERBURY, FELICITY GORDON-WALKER. She is a tall, thin lesbian of 55 whose frenzied movements reveal her neurotic and insecure character. She falls over herself to please even those who despise her. She advocates a globalist religion which is non-judgmental and which places Christianity on the same level as all others. She is one of the elites in the Anglican Church who took Christ completely out of it.

WILLIAM BUTLER, THE CEO OF INTERNATIONAL OIL AND GAS. Butler is American, 55, a fit and handsome man. He heads the biggest oil company in the world and is aware of his immense power, especially over governments. His company want a quick end to the civil war in Bengara-even at the cost of the eradication of the Christian enclave. Right and wrong play no part in his decision making- the maximization of profit does.

PIPPA WINTHROP. The wife of Sir Hugh Winthrop. Pippa is 63, a shallow and selfish person who indulges her taste for gourmet cuisine and fine wines. She is a "new socialist" who rejects the frugality of Labour's founders. Her understanding of the world is rudimentary.

AVERY FOREST. He is the American ambassador to Britain who exercises great power over the Prime Minister. His urbane manner is a mask for his ruthlessness.

Author's Notes

THE SETTINGS. The accounts of all stage settings are deliberately sparse so that the director and set designer can visualize the scenes as they think appropriate.

THE TIME. The action of this play is set in the mid-nineties when Blair was Prime Minister and gay marriage and the woke ideology were given official blessing. Most prominent amongst the tenets of the "new religion" were the decrees that all faiths were of equal value and that all types of sexual perversion were permissible.

The actual time of the genocidal war was between 1967 and 1970. It was a crime against humanity that was permitted by western governments, especially the left-wing administration of Harold Wilson, the Prime Minister of Britain. His failure to act in defense of the Biafran people symbolized the fall of Great Britain in the realm of morality and national honor.

In a very real sense, this surrender of Judeo-Christian morality was responsible for the genocide of the Biafran people, for without reverence for its precepts of right and wrong, the mass murder of Christians became permissible. That which was evil and wrong was sanctioned by a non-judgmental and perfidious acceptance of abominable crimes. Faced with the massacre of Christian people by Muslim armies, Sir Winston Churchill would have sent British forces to prevent it. He revered Judeo-Christian civilization and described Islam as "...the most retrograde force in the world."

Wilson and the British leaders who followed him worshipped at the shrine of the perverse and the absurd, promoting Islam as the "religion of peace..." Islam of the most radical kind was unleashed against the Christian Biafrans, and it was deemed acceptable by Wilson, his friends in the Soviet Union, and the deluded leaders of the western world. This rejection of Judeo-Christian morality and duty matured when Blair came to power, and it has dominated British and western political affairs since then. By design, it dominates in the play as strongly in the time of the Biafra War as it did in the 90's.

ACT 1, SCENE 1.

THE OFFICE OF THE BRITISH FOREIGN SECRETARY, SIR HUGH WINTHROP. THE FURNISHINGS ARE VICTORIAN, AND SOMBRE PORTRAITS OF PAST FOREIGN SECRETARIES ADORN THE WALLS. THERE IS A LARGE DESK AT CENTER STAGE WITH A CHAIR BEHIND IT. A PHONE AND A PA SYSTEM ARE SITUATED ON THE TOP OF THE DESK, ALONG WITH BASKETS FILLED WITH FILES. A 1990'S COMPUTER IS ON THE DESK. TWO CHAIRS ARE SITUATED IN FRONT OF THE DESK.

Sir Hugh is a dapper 63, dressed in a dark business suit. He is well groomed and a bit paunchy. He paces in front of the desk, hands behind his back, his expression one of concern. He mumbles...

SIR HUGH: I told him...I told him... Damn, the man!

    (He picks up a newspaper from the desk and glances at the front page)

    It had to happen!

    (He throws the paper forcefully on the desk)

    Damn him!

    (There is a knocking on the door)

SIR HUGH: Come in!

    (JAMES DONALD, HIS AIDE, walks in. He is tall, handsome, and athletic. He exudes a quiet confidence. He wears a conventional dark pin-stripe suit.)

JAMES DONALD: Good morning, Minister, you're early today.

(His accent is distinctly upper class)

SIR HUGH: Yes, I've hardly slept, James, I've a lot on my mind...

(His accent is educated working class from the North of England)

I hope the traffic wasn't heavy?

JAMES DONALD: Just the usual mess on the M-25...one lane shut down.

SIR HUGH: Some totally unnecessary road work, I suppose?

JAMES DONALD: Well, a lorry broke down and blocked one lane.

SIR HUGH: Too many of those bloody things on the road if you ask me! All those monsters coming here from the European Union. One of the dubious benefits of joining it. Their drivers couldn't care less about our traffic laws.

JAMES DONALD: I think they'll comply as time goes on...there's always hope, isn't there?

SIR HUGH: Hmm...You're an incorrigible optimist, James. Not a bad attitude to have in the grim world of foreign affairs. (Beat)

JAMES DONALD: Have you read the early editions, Sir?

SIR HUGH: Yes, I have! This... (picks the paper up) is in the Herald. They're blaming us, a socialist government, for the bloodbath in Bengara! They've singled me out for their most biting criticism as the Foreign Secretary! I mean...here...look at the headline: "Over two thousand civilians killed in the last week..." The mass casualties, I might add, are from heavy artillery...

JAMES DONALD: One hundred-&-fifty-five-millimeter howitzers, which we supplied to the Bengaran government...

SIR HUGH (enraged): The Prime Minister authorized the delivery of those weapons against my considered advice. I warned him that those artillery pieces could cause mass casualties.

JAMES DONALD: If I remember correctly, his argument was that we always supply military materiel to the armed forces of our former colonies. He added that if we didn't, the Russians would.

SIR HUGH: He was right, of course... The damn Russians will get their foot in the door at the slightest opportunity. But, we could have given the Bengaran government lighter stuff. We've got warehouses full of 25 -pounders from the Korean War! I also suggested financial incentives to placate the Bengaran government.

JAMES DONALD: Well Sir, the democratically- elected government we left behind after independence was deposed by a military junta. We're now dealing with an Islamic dictatorship. They believe that their "god" has given them absolute authority to subject all non-Muslims in Bengara to Islamic sharia law-and to forcibly convert them to Islam. The Christians in Benugu refused to comply and so became the enemies of the junta. General Amir Khan, the leader of the junta has pledged to enforce the conversion of the Christians... Resistance will be met with death.

**SIR HUGH
(aghast):** Death? Death? For refusing to become Muslim? They want to wipe out the entire Christian population? That's outrageous! Barbaric! (Beat)

JAMES DONALD: Sir, it's become clear that the Muslim junta want to gain complete control of the Christian enclave. I've done some research into the Benugu enclave...It has always been semi-autonomous. The tribes there were a coastal people, shrewd traders, and open to what western civilization had to offer. When we arrived, their leaders accepted Christianity, introduced mainly by missionaries from the Catholic, Presbyterian and Anglican churches. The Christian tribal elders actually helped us to end the slave trade, which was controlled by the more numerous Muslim tribes. That collaboration caused much of the enmity between the Muslims and the Benugan Christians. Historically, the rebellions we had to deal with there were instigated by the Muslim tribes. They rejected western civilization and its values.

SIR HUGH: I do recall reading about those insurrections... The Muslims did finally submit- after we courted their leaders with money to compensate them for their losses in the slave trade.

JAMES DONALD: Yes, Sir...their allegiance was conditional on "incentives." The allegiance of the Benugan Christians, on the other hand, was rooted in our common faith and values. I have to say that we always favored the Christian population in their disputes with their Muslim neighbors. This, of course, led to tribal skirmishes.

SIR HUGH: Skirmishes which have now developed into a full-scale war! (He looks at the article again)

SIR HUGH
(cont. looks at article): ...This says that over a half a million Benugans died last year. Now, the Muslim junta has asked the Russians to supply them with night fighters and fighter bombers! They don't need them! They already outnumber the Benugans by six-to-one...they've got our heavy artillery. Why has it taken them so long to win a decisive victory?

JAMES DONALD: They're fighting in dense jungle, Minister. Large infantry formations are subject to constant ambushes. Artillery is hard to direct against camouflaged targets. They need these Russian fighters to bomb the Benugans into submission. They have no defenses against air attack. (Silence)

SIR HUGH: They'll probably bomb the main population centers to bring the Benugans to their knees. Port Victoria has about three million inhabitants.

JAMES DONALD: The Christian forces in Port Victoria are finding it extremely difficult to get supplied by sea. Two of their cargo vessels were recently sunk at sea-probably Russian sabotage. If it weren't for supplies coming in from the hinterland Port Victoria would be starved out.

SIR HUGH: My God, this is all very disturbing... We've got the national press hounding us. They can turn public opinion against the government! This is devolving into a genocide! The Prime Minister has known about this impending catastrophe for a year, and he has sidelined my warnings. We can't leave millions of innocent people to bombed and starved to death!

JAMES DONALD: I agree, Minister. We have a responsibility to intervene in a country we created. The media is demanding answers, and talking heads on The BBC have accused the Foreign Office of facilitating a genocide.

SIR HUGH: What? Have they gone bloody mad? They're accusing the Foreign Office of facilitating a genocide?

JAMES DONALD: I know it's absurd, Sir-even for the BBC... The media, however, can't be ignored.

SIR HUGH: I'd like to sue them, but that would be a waste of time. The Prime Minister bears the responsibility for all this! He's ignored all my warnings and is focused on becoming the next superstar of The European Union. He's infatuated with being the voice of the brave new world the globalists in Brussels are planning. The man wants to pretend that we never had an empire or the Commonwealth that succeeded it.

(Silence)

...We'll have to act within the purview of the Foreign Office.

JAMES DONALD: We're not exactly powerless, Sir.

SIR HUGH: Can we talk to the representatives of both sides in this war?

JAMES DONALD: I've opened communications with General Musa, the ambassador of Bangura. He's willing to meet with you at your request. The ambassador of Benugu...

**SIR HUGH
(interrupts):**   ...Ambassador? They have an embassy in London? We haven't given them diplomatic status yet. How can they afford to maintain an embassy?

JAMES DONALD: Well, they call it their embassy. It's actually a small office in Earl's Court. They have a skeleton staff and keep a very low profile. They don't want to provoke General Musa. He's got a well-earned reputation for brutality.

SIR HUGH: Really? This is England; he can't break the law here.

JAMES DONALD: Well, apparently, he can. Two Benugans who condemned the atrocities of the Muslim junta on television vanished without a trace. Scotland Yard has not been able to locate them. A contact of mine at the Yard thinks that General Musa was behind their disappearance. Several of the General's thugs have been detained for assaulting his critics.

SIR HUGH
(angered):   These uncivilized barbarians are abusing diplomatic privileges! They should all be summarily deported! They apparently have no respect for our laws and customs, and they don't belong here. I'm afraid that when power is given to the leaders of some of our former colonies, it elicits their worst primitive behavior. Makes me wonder if the Commonwealth is an absurd fabrication.

JAMES DONALD: Perhaps, Sir...but we're talking about a rogue minority who abuse our privileges. The majority respect them.

SIR HUGH
(apologetic):   Yes...yes, I take your point... In spite of the many challenges we face, we must continue to devote ourselves to the Commonwealth ideal. We have to nurture the leaders who care about their people and not their bank accounts. What about the fellow from Benugu-their ambassador?

JAMES DONALD: His name is Tony Nwokedi. He's around 35 and has an unusual history. His father was a sergeant in the Bengaran army when independence was declared. We selected him for officer training at Sandhurst because he showed promise.

SIR HUGH: We did a lot of that sort of thing to set up the armed forces of the new Commonwealth nations.

JAMES DONALD: While he was stationed here, he married a Jamaican woman who was also a serving soldier. They had a son, "Tony." They wanted him to have the full benefits of a British education. They sent him to posh prep schools and then to Winchester.

SIR HUGH: Winchester? My word, they must have been well heeled!

JAMES DONALD: His family were successful traders and bankers in Benugu.

SIR HUGH: How did he do at Winchester?

JAMES DONALD: He proved to be a brilliant scholar and a good batsman. He played for the first eleven, in fact.

SIR HUGH: Good man! You know, I played for the first eleven at my grammar school in Leeds. I can say with pride that I scored a century once. Well, I always manage to get along with fellow cricketers.

JAMES DONALD: Tony Nwokedi also played for the first eleven at Saint Catherine's College at Oxford. He graduated at 21 with a degree in economics.

SIR HUGH: Very impressive! I suppose he spent his holidays visiting his parents in Bengara?

JAMES DONALD: Yes, he went home whenever he could. His father rose to be the Secretary of Defense.

SIR HUGH: A family of high achievers. I suppose they lost everything when the civil war began?

JAMES DONALD: I'm afraid both his parents were dragged out of bed and shot when the Muslim junta staged their coup. Mr. Nwokedi was fortunately in Britain when it happened...

(Silence)

SIR HUGH: Poor chap... You know, he sounds like a decent sort. When can he be here?

JAMES DONALD: You've got a cabinet meeting at three. What about tomorrow morning, at ten? You'll have time to read the early reports from overseas before he arrives.

SIR HUGH: Yes, that will work, thank you. You know, I've held this office for almost five years...It's taught me a lot about diplomacy. It's a thankless task. The politicians always find a way to blame us for their mistakes.

JAMES DONALD: And we can't really fight back, can we? They make the minefields and then send us to diffuse them.

SIR HUGH: Couldn't have put it better myself. This conflict in Bengara is a minefield, James...I wonder if we'll survive it?

ACT I, SCENE II.

OFFICE OF THE FOREIGN SECRETARY. MORNING.

The FOREIGN SECRETARY is standing at his desk perusing documents and the screen of his computer. There is a knocking on the door. James Donald enters with TONY NWOKEDI, the Ambassador of Benugu. He is dressed in a dark business suit, a blue shirt, and a red tie. He is around 35, tall, handsome and athletic.

JAMES DONALD: Good morning, Sir Hugh. Allow me to introduce Tony Nwokedi, the representative of Benugu.

SIR HUGH: Ah, Mr. Nwokedi, it is a pleasure to meet you. (they shake hands) Please take a seat. Can we offer you anything to drink?

TONY NWOKEDI: No, thank you, Sir Hugh.
(His accent is English upper class. (JAMES DONALD AND NWOKEDI SIT)

SIR HUGH: Mr. Donald, my Under-Secretary, has given me a glowing account of your career as a batsman. I understand that you were an outstanding player at Winchester and St. Catherine's?

TONY NWOKEDI: Well, I spent a lot of time in the nets to attain competence. I simply loved cricket, Sir Hugh.

SIR HUGH: And one does excel at what one loves. You know, I wasn't a bad batsman myself...made a century at my grammar school.

TONY NWOKEDI: Making a century is no mean accomplishment.

SIR HUGH: Actually, one of the high points of my life.

TONY NWOKEDI:	I must thank you for giving me this opportunity to discuss the situation in my country.
SIR HUGH:	Well, Mr. Nwokedi, we must try to end the hostilities which are taking so many innocent lives.
TONY NWOKEDI:	Mr. Donald has informed me that you recently evaluated the articles in the major newspapers concerning the rising death toll.
JAMES DONALD:	Mainly the articles in the Guardian and the Times.
SIR HUGH:	They were very discouraging and most uncomplimentary to me and the Foreign Office! I want to assure you that I have tried to...minimize the damage to your country, as far as I was able. I am appalled at the carnage that is being wrought.

(beat)

TONY NWOKEDI:	Sir Hugh, I've just heard from my military attaché that the Russians have delivered a squadron of night fighters to the military junta in Bengara... They will soon be reinforced by fighter-bombers for daylight missions.
SIR HUGH:	My word...we didn't think that would happen so soon... James, your thoughts?
JAMES DONALD:	I believe the night fighters are Mig-29s, Sir. The Bangaran junta don't have the pilots to fly them, so the Russians have probably provided them as part of their arms package.

TONY NWOKEDI: They're mercenary pilots, Mr. Donald. Our agents have seen them in the bars of Owerra, the capital of Bengara. They're mainly from East Germany and Bulgaria.

JAMES DONALD: Renegades who have no remorse about killing civilians. We've seen them in action in the Congo and Sudan. They decimated those countries with indiscriminate bombing.

TONY NWOKEDI: They'll fly the night fighters, and we'll be helpless to stop them. We depend totally on the flights sent by the Red Cross and Caritas International...they come in at night. They use the last functioning airport we have near Port Victoria. The Russian Migs will pick them off. When the fighter-bombers become operational, they'll bomb Port Victoria to rubble.

SIR HUGH: Total air superiority will also enable the junta's land forces to advance right up to the outskirts of Port Victoria... They'll be able to use their heavy artillery against the city...We're facing a human catastrophe.

TONY NWOKEDI: Call it genocide, Sir Hugh.

(Silence).

JAMES DONALD: After the war started a year ago, we tried to temper the military ambitions of General Amir Khan, the president of Muslim junta. We offered generous financial incentives, which the Prime Minister approved.

SIR HUGH: Fifty million pounds in foreign aid, and it turned out to be a fiasco. The money vanished into thin air.

TONY NWOKEDI.
(laughs)   I know that General Amir Khan used that money to pay for some ammunition shipments. But most of it went into his Swiss bank account.

JAMES DONALD: Our consulate in Marseille informed me that General Khan recently bought a villa in Juan les Pins for ten million euros. He also has a yacht moored in Monaco.

SIR HUGH: What bloody cheek! We stipulated that the aid was for new schools and hospitals! Don't these people have any sense of decency?

TONY NWOKEDI: Their sense of "decency" or, in broader terms, "morality" contrasts radically from our own, Sir Hugh. By that, I mean our Judeo- Christian morality and values. "Do unto other you would be done by them" is fundamental to Judeo-Christian civilization. This golden rule is alien to the Islamic civilization of General Amir Khan.

SIR HUGH: I'm afraid I don't understand, Mr. Nwokedi. I have always believed that all men...all religions...share basic values...Like being decent to one another.

TONY NWOKEDI: To the religious Muslim, all non-Muslims are "kuffar..." Infidels. We are, by the command of the Koran, their enemies. The Muslims are taught from infancy that the infidel has to be subdued slain that we are their inferiors. A core teaching of the Koran is Sura 48:29.... "Mohammed is Allah's apostle. Those who follow him are ruthless to the unbelievers but merciful to one another..." So, you see, Sir Hugh, the Islamic "god" is very different from the God we follow. Muslims can show compassion and mercy to one another but not to Christians. General Amir Khan is bound to obey this command, which allows him and his soldiers to rape, plunder, and massacre...It allows him to break any and all treaties with the infidel... Your overtures of peace, your "incentives," are treated with contempt.

                      (Silence)

SIR HUGH: Mr. Nwokedi, if what you say is true, and I don't doubt that it is...this ideology, this "religion..." is an existential threat to the world order we created after the Second World War. It rejects the possibility of cooperation with all non-Muslim peoples...It wants to shape the world to fit its own intolerant beliefs...James, have you made a study of it?

JAMES DONALD: Not really, Sir. I should have made a more thorough examination of its theology. it. I'll catch up...

SIR HUGH: From what you tell us, Mr. Nwokedi, General Amir Khan is taking our largesse with one hand and stabbing us in the back with the other.

TONY NWOKEDI: Succinctly put, Sir Hugh.

JAMES DONALD: I have to conclude that we're dealing with people who have complete scorn for our values...

TONY NWOKEDI (interrupts): ...but who pretend that they accept them when convenient... As Mohammed taught, "...war is deceit," and the Muslims are taught to be accomplished masters of it.

SIR HUGH: We must face the harsh fact that the Junta's objective is to destroy Port Victoria...and there's little we can do to stop them...

(Beat)

TONY NWOKEDI: Sir Hugh, where only force can stop force, I recommend that the British government equip us with anti-aircraft missiles. If we can shoot down the Russian night fighters, we can continue to be supplied by air. That would give us breathing space. I can tell you in confidence that the French are willing to supply us with light tanks and mobile field artillery...If we get them, we can beat back the junta's army and force a stalemate. The French, however, won't make a move unless...

**SIR HUGH
(interrupting):**   ...unless we knock out the Russian fighters first.

TONY NWOKEDI: Exactly... They are ready to drive the weapons south from their Sub- Saharan territories, but they won't expose their convoys to air attack.

**SIR HUGH
(annoyed):**   Trust the French not to tell us anything! They've got to have some ulterior motive. What do they want, Mr. Nwokedi?

TONY NWOKEDI: A share of our oil, Sir.

SIR HUGH: Ah yes, that's to be expected, of course. You never get anything for nothing, do you?

TONY NWOKEDI: Oil is the only card we have to play, Sir Hugh.

SIR HUGH: And it's a trump card... if you can control the oil... What are your expectations at this juncture?

TONY NWOKEDI: Not sanguine... We've already lost over a half million people. The Bengaran junta have allowed their soldiers to rape and debauch our women and children. Entire villages have been burned to the ground... Their inhabitants were herded into churches, which were then incinerated... Heavy artillery fire has forced us to keep retreating to fresh defensive lines...We've retreated all the way to Port Victoria, and now we've got our backs to the sea. If we don't get anti-aircraft missiles soon, we can't hold on... I estimate that we have two weeks left before our resistance collapses. A bloodbath will inevitably follow.

JAMES DONALD: Minister, it's a slim hope, but could we pressure the United Nations to send a peacekeeping force?

SIR HUGH
(skeptical):   Have they ever worked? Their African efforts were fiascos.

TONY NWOKEDI: The UN is controlled by the Russians and the Organization for Islamic Cooperation...56 Muslim nations which form a solid voting bloc. They will never sanction a peacekeeping force to prevent their Muslim allies in Bengara from winning a war against Christians.

(Silence)

SIR HUGH: Is there anybody helping you now, Mr. Nwokedi?

TONY NWOKEDI: Caritas, the Catholic Relief Organization, the Red Cross, and the Anglican Church. They operate the relief flights.

JAMES DONALD: What about the Vatican? Since Caritas is involved?

TONY NWOKEDI: The Pope has tried through diplomatic channels to stop the looting and burning of churches and the mass killing of Christians. His intervention made matters worse. You see, the Muslim junta saw nis efforts as an affront to Islam... The Pope is their arch enemy.

SIR HUGH: What about the Church of England?

TONY NWOKEDI: They send a relief plane every month...that's all.

JAMES DONALD: I understand that the Church of England's Board of Directors decided not to provoke the junta by going beyond their.... "token" relief effort.

SIR HUGH: I would have thought that they would have cared more about saving their flock in Benugu than about appeasing their persecutors...

TONY NWOKEDI: Sir, if we don't get the military help we need, there won't be a church or its congregation left. We need the anti-aircraft missiles now.

                        (Silence).

SIR HUGH: Mr. Nwokedi I can only express my deep sadness at the plight of your people. I know that the British government will have to take action soon...or Port Victoria will fall, and thousands will die.

TONY NWOKEDI: I therefore implore you, Sir Hugh, to impress on the Prime Minister that we will be slaughtered without the missiles. Royal Air Force Hercules transports can deliver them to Port Victoria in twelve hours.

JAMES DONALD: Yes, they can refuel on the island of Fernando Po...we have a base there.

SIR HUGH: Well then, if it can be done, then let's bloody well do it! James, arrange an emergency meeting with the Prime Minister-at his earliest convenience.

JAMES DONALD: I will, Sir. Mr. Nwokedi we will do everything possible to help you.

TONY NWOKEDI: Thank you, Mr. Donald, I trust that you will.

SIR HUGH
(rising):   Well, let's get a move on, eh? Mr. Nwokedi it has been a great pleasure meeting you. I understand you read economics at Oxford?

TONY NWOKEDI: Yes, Sir. I wanted to go on to a Ph.D. but my father prevailed on me to join the family business.

SIR HUGH: I'm sure you'll restore it after this awful war has ended. I do admire your courage...and devotion to your country. I will meet with the Prime Minister and strongly recommend that we provide the missiles. We'll be in touch soon.

(They shake hands).

JAMES DONALD: I'll walk with you to your car, Mr. Nwokedi.

TONY NWOKEDI: Oh, there's no need, I took the tube to Westminster. Thank you so much, Mr. Donald.

JAMES DONALD: I hope we have better news the next time we meet.

TONY NWOKEDI: Goodbye, Sir.

(He exits. James Donald walks up to the desk of Sir Hugh)

JAMES DONALD: I'll call Downing Street. There's no time to waste. We have a profound responsibility to the population of Benugu. We can't stand by and let the junta's forces overrun them.

SIR HUGH
(sighs): It's a near hopeless situation, James, and all we can do is take the next step...Secure a meeting with the PM.

JAMES DONALD: I will, Sir. About meeting with the other side. Shall I facilitate a conference with General Musa?

SIR HUGH: Yes... He's a vile man, and I'm not looking forward to meeting him. If I had my way, I'd deport him...and his entire bloody staff!

ACT 1, SCENE III.

A BENCH IN THE GARDEN OF THE FOREIGN SECRETARY'S HAMPSTEAD HOME. IT IS EVENING, SIR HUGH AND HIS WIFE, PIPPA, SIT TOGETHER SIPPING WINE. A SMALL TABLE IS SITUATED IN FRONT OF THEM, ON WHICH RESTS A BOTTLE OF CABERNET SAUVIGNON. STRAINS OF CHOPIN'S NOCTURNE NUMBER 9 ARE HEARD.

(The music fades out)

SIR HUGH: Chopin is such a tragic figure...how a man who suffered so much could rise above it all and create such beauty is beyond me. He defied the futility of life. And the repulsiveness humanity can sink to.

PIPPA (laughs in a silly way): Oh, come on, Hugh, it couldn't have been all that bad?

He had a devoted mistress and spent a lot of time in the South of France. Do you like the new roses I planted? They're cuts from the Butchart Gardens, you know.

SIR HUGH: Oh, they're lovely...all the way from Vancouver Island. The hollyhocks are looking splendid, Pippa.

PIPPA: Yes, it's amazing what sunshine and fertilizer can do! I'm using loads from my compost heap...must be ecologically correct, mustn't we?

SIR HUGH
(bored with her):   Yes...we mustn't add to the distress of all our green friends. They carry such a heavy burden of responsibility for the planet.

PIPPA: Oh, come on! They are improving the health of the planet!

(Beat)

The tiger cannas are flourishing, aren't they? They're incorrigible...like me, I suppose?

(She giggles)

SIR HUGH: Yes, I received the last invoice from Fortnum and Masons...it's over a thousand pounds, and the one from Harrods's is frightening! You really should stop emptying our bank account.

PIPPA: Well Hugh dear, we are the premier diplomatic family in the country, and we do have to entertain. We host the dignitaries of the most important nations in the world. Our cocktail parties and dinners have to be, as the French say, "Comme il foot." (She mispronounces "faut."). As for the expense, I simply cannot manage without the best catering companies in London! Our prestige is of paramount importance, you'll agree?

SIR HUGH
(sighs):   We have to do it, I suppose, but it's such a damn waste. Apart from anything else, I detest most of the people we have to entertain. Their insincerity is insufferable.

PIPPA:

Well, a lot of these heads of states from the Third World are still...dare I say it, unrefined? We'll just have to teach them good table manners, that's all.

SIR HUGH:

Just table manners? If you ask me, our efforts to civilize and improve seem to be a lost cause...Some of them will always be crude and savage...because they want to be.

**PIPPA
(shocked):**

What? I never expected to hear that from a lifelong socialist like you! You were always so confident that we could elevate humanity to a new world of enlightenment and international understanding.

SIR HUGH:

Well, it appears that some of these leaders from the Third World despise our vision for a better, kinder humanity. They prefer their old, senseless, and brutal ways. Our aspirations for a world built on rational thought and altruistic values have no appeal to those with malevolent instincts.

PIPPA:

Goodness me! From what you say, they sound like the Nazis!

SIR HUGH:

No, not Nazis...We knew what we were dealing with when they emerged from the gutter. Hitler very obligingly spelled out his intentions... Mein Kamph, the Sudetenland occupation, Czechoslovakia...We understood Hitler and his agenda. We are now facing a hostile force that is more dangerous than Nazism...one we've never faced before... one we hardly understand.

PIPPA: I'm completely in the dark as to what you're talking about, dear.

SIR HUGH: It's a "spiritual" force, with a "god" that commands absolute belief on pain of death...A god who commands his followers to murder all those who refuse to believe in him.

(Beat)

PIPPA
(gulps her drink): Well, with this "god" and all, it sounds like you're dealing with a cult... Surely you can suppress them without much fuss?

SIR HUGH: Unfortunately, this "god"_ is worshipped by two billion people on this earth... They've been dormant up till now, but like demons from hell, they've been released to ravage and kill. This cult, as you call it, is the biggest challenge we face as a civilization...because presently, we're at a loss to comprehend it.

PIPPA: Well, if you ask me, Hugh, you only have choices... Either you ignore it, in the hope that it will fizzle out-or you can squash it! That's what we have the army for, isn't it?

SIR HUGH: I am not authorized to deploy our forces, my dear...I'm just the Foreign Secretary...As you must be aware, our government's policy for decades has been to avoid military conflict at all costs...some may call it a policy of cowardice...We've encouraged tyrants through our dereliction of duty to uphold international law...

PIPPA: Well, staying out of these futile wars in countries we've never heard of makes sense to me! Our boys won't die senselessly.

(Beat)

What a gorgeous sunset, Hugh... Pour me another glass, would you, dear?

ACT II, SCENE I.

THE OFFICE OF GENERAL MUSA, THE AMBASSADOR OF BENGARA, THE WALLS ARE FESTOONED WITH AFRICAN MASKS, MOUNTED HEADS OF GAME ANIMALS, ATROCIOUS PAINTINGS OF FRUIT BASKETS AND FLOWERS.

GENERAL MUSA SITS BEHIND A HUGE DESK, HIS FACE HIDDEN BEHIND A SOFT PORN MAGAZINE WHICH DISPLAYS A WHITE WOMAN IN A PROVOCATIVE POSE. HE MAKES LITTLE GRUNTS OF APPROVAL AS HE TURNS A PAGE. THE ONLY DOOR IS DOWNSTAGE AND TO THE STAGE RIGHT.

THERE IS A KNOCKING ON THE DOOR. BIN MUSA THROWS THE MAGAZINE ON THE TABLE. HE IS CLEARLY ANNOYED...

GENERAL MUSA: Who is it?

AFRICAN MALE

VOICE (V.O.):   The Foreign Secretary and his Aide, Sir.

GENERAL MUSA:	Make them wait!
	(He gets up and stretches. He is a large and obese man of average height and ugly.) He walks to a mirror on the S/L wall and preens himself. He gets his hat from the rack near the door and puts it on. He walks to the mirror again, checks himself out, and then approaches the door. His general's uniform is bizarre and gaudy. He sits at his desk and bellows:
	All right, show them in now!
	(The door opens, and the Foreign Secretary and James Donald Walk in. The door closes behind them)
SIR HUGH:	Good morning, General Musa, I've wanted to meet you ever since you were appointed ambassador
GENERAL MUSA (laughs):	Oh really? Most British officials try to avoid me. I suppose they believe all the lies the British press publish about me.
SIT HUGH:	No doubt published in the yellow press. My Aide. Mr. Donald tells me that you were once a sergeant in the colonial British army?
GENERAL MUSA:	Oh yes, decades ago-during your occupation of my country
JAMES DONALD:	You were decorated for valor if I'm not mistaken?

GENERAL MUSA: It was just a commendation on, not a medal. African soldiers were not awarded medals in those days...we were just used for all the dirty jobs. I killed a lot of enemy soldiers... As a matter of fact, I used the heads of prisoners as footballs....

(He laughs crudely)

...You see, the enemy made a big mistake when they killed my brother. He was a corporal in my platoon. I took his death very badly, and as they say…heads had to roll...

(He laughs with obscene delight)

SIR HUGH: I see... Your measures were certainly "drastic..."

GENERAL MUSA: Prisoners are such a logistical problem; you'll agree Sir Hugh? I spared mine the humiliation of captivity. Please, do sit down.

(They sit in the two chairs in front of his desk.) I won't offer you anything to drink because I know you want to get down to business. We're all busy men, after all....

SIR HUGH: Well, yes general, we are. I gather from intelligence that the war in Bengara has reached a critical stage. Your forces have dealt the opposition...

GENERAL MUSA
(enraged):

"Opposition?" Rebels, traitors, that's what we call them! They will pay with their lives for betraying my country. We are going to destroy those bastards, every one of them. Am I making myself clear?

(Silence. Sir Hugh and James Donald are taken aback by his violent reaction.)

SIR HUGH:

General Musa, your country was a colony of Great Britain for over a hundred years. We have the utmost respect for the people of Bengara and want to prevent...

GENERAL MUSA
(interrupts):

..."Prevent?" You mean interfere! If that's why you're here, you're wasting your time.

JAMES DONALD:

General Musa, you must know that Britain gives your country more than fifty million pounds in foreign aid every year. We built and staff your universities and health service. We're now building the new airport near Owerra, the capital. I am sure that your president, General Amir Khan, wants to continue our cordial relationship.

GENERAL MUSA:

You're sure of nothing, Donald... You've come here to beg.

(He laughs)

You think I'm a fool? I have intelligence sources, too-in, London! I know that you met with the "ambassador" of Bhengu yesterday... You're here at his request.

JAMES DONALD: We're here because we have a moral responsibility to prevent a human catastrophe in your country.

GENERAL MUSA: Oh, you must mean the coming annihilation of our enemies in Port Victoria? After a year of pursuing them, we've cornered the rats...and now we're going to finish them-and end the war. You want peace? Good, this is how we'll give it to you-over their dead bodies!

SIR HUGH: The lives of three million inhabitants are at risk, general. If we're here to beg, we're begging on their behalf. You don't have to wipe out an entire population.

GENERAL MUSA (chuckling): I suppose we can be generous and spare a few...especially all their voluptuous women. That aside, the final assault must go forward. There are at least fifty thousand Benugan soldiers holed up in Port Victoria.

JAMES DONALD: They're desperately short of food, and they're running out of ammunition. They can't last long against the kind of attack your army will mount.

GENERAL MUSA: But...they are good fighters...I'll give them that, no question. They've killed over two hundred thousand of our soldiers since the war started! But we've beaten them back, thanks to the heavy artillery your prime minister supplied to us... Oh yes, if there's blame to go around for the killing, you're entitled to a big share of it.

(Silence)

SIR HUGH: We may have supplied those weapons... you used them-without regard for the civilian population!

GENERAL MUSA
(enraged):   You British make me sick! With one hand, you make money supplying the arms that annihilate thousands, and with the other, you come holding an olive branch begging us for mercy... You know, I've learned a lot from you...I'm a savage, born that way, and by choice...but my brutality is out in the open for the whole world to see. And I don't apologize for it... Yours comes gift-wrapped in good manners and... Hypocrisy.

SIR HUGH: I want to emphasize that I was against supplying your junta with the heavy artillery. Since you so proudly call yourself a savage, I did perceive that there were enough of your kind to use those weapons to cause mass casualties. The Prime Minister, against my strongest advice, sent two hundred artillery pieces to your president, General Amir Khan... What we have to do now is to make those guns go silent. We need a ceasefire. The final victory is yours. We concede that... General Musa, there are many ways to meet your demands without more carnage.

GENERAL MUSA: And what would they be, Sir Hugh?

SIR HUGH: We could evacuate all the fighting men from Port Victoria, the ones who pose a threat to you. We can do this under UN supervision.

JAMES DONALD: We'll arrange their passage to a neutral country-and we'll bear the cost. The remaining population in Port Victoria will be unarmed civilians...There needn't be a bloodbath.

SIR HUGH: We can place a UN peacekeeping force to police the city while we organize the total evacuation of the population. You will lose nothing by exercising restraint...

(Beat)

GENERAL MUSA: Well, what you say does sound good, but it's too good to be true. You see, the Benugan soldiers are fanatical Christians. They will never stop fighting us. They'll organize guerilla campaigns from abroad. They won't hesitate to assassinate the leaders of my country-including me! This is a war that can only be won when one side is completely wiped out by the other...We don't want to take Port Victoria and the rest of the Christian enclave just to be administrators...We want to dominate it, control it, make it an integral part of Bengara...leaving no one who can stab us in the back.

(Silence)

SIR HUGH: You're saying that the Benugan Christians must be wiped out... (He explodes)

That's an outrage against humanity! We won't tolerate that! I'm taking this to the level of heads of state! Surely you don't speak for your president and the junta?

GENERAL MUSA: Even I don't have such a big ego as to advocate a policy which opposes that of my superiors. Foreign Secretary, what I have told you is the policy of my president and the junta. I am simply carrying it out.

(Beat)

SIR HUGH: I'll be taking this up with the Prime Minister. I have tried to reason with you, General Musa, but you apparently are slighting me.

GENERAL MUSA: You tried to sway me, but you failed... Don't be too hard on yourself. Foreign Secretary, you're just a go-between with no power. I do sympathize with your predicament. You have to deal with diplomatic subtleties, with imagined possibilities, with your "moral" prohibitions. But look, please do talk to your prime minister, and if he can confer with General Amir Khan, my president, and have my orders changed-I'll have to obey them, won't I? I am under authority.

SIR HUGH: It's a great pity that you are not commanded by the authority of mercy, General...James, I believe we need to leave now.

(They both rise)

JAMES DONALD: This has been a very illuminating meeting, General bin Musa. You've made your policy starkly clear...It's genocide by any other name.

GENERAL MUSA: Have a nice day, gentlemen. Mr. Donald, in parting, let me say that "genocide" is often misused to describe something very simple-a political necessity!

ACT II, SCENE II.

THE PRIME MINISTER'S OFFICE. PORTRAITS OF PAST PRIME MINISTERS ADORN THE WALLS. THERE ARE TWO LANDSCAPES BY TURNER. HIS LARGE DESK AT STAGE CENTER DOMINATES THE ROOM, THE DOOR IS SITUATED AT DOWNSTAGE/RIGHT. THE PHONE RINGS, AND HE PICKS IT UP. HE IS AROUND 60. HARRY CROSSMAN IS A LARGE MAN WHOSE MANNER IS OVERBEARING. HIS ACCENT IS "NORTHERN," WORKING CLASS.

PRIME MINISTER: Yes, yes, send him in!

(The door opens, and Sir Hugh enters)

SIR HUGH: Good afternoon, Prime Minister. Thank you for seeing me at such short notice.

PRIME MINISTER: I finished reading your report late last night...it was viscerally depressing, Hugh. I had no idea the situation had deteriorated so badly in Bengara. It looks like we're on the precipice of a human disaster.

SIR HUGH: The junta's forces are within fifty miles of Port Victoria, and we don't have much time or options open to us.

PRIME MINISTER: Your report left me in no doubt as to the urgency of the situation. I've been up half the bloody night trying to phone General Amir Khan in Owerra. He won't take my calls!

SIR HUGH: I'm sorry, Prime Minister.

PRIME MINISTER:	His secretary told me that he was "indisposed" and that I had to deal with General Musa in London. Apparently, Musa has complete authority to speak for the president.
SIR HUGH:	General Musa presents an enormous problem, I'm afraid. I bore the full brunt of his hostility yesterday.
PRIME MINISTER:	I've learned about him through MI-6... Did you know that he's married to the president's sister?
SIR HUGH:	Wouldn't surprise me. I understand that in their culture, they keep power in the family.
PRIME MINISTER:	Ah yes, their "culture..." We know so little about it-to our disadvantage, and I hate to be surprised! I wish MI-6 had kept me up to date on the progress of the ground war.
SIR HUGH:	I met with Tony Nwokedi yesterday. He's the representative of the Christian enclave of Benugu. He was able to inform me of the latest battlefield developments.
PRIME MINISTER:	How did he manage that?

SIR HUGH: His military attaché has established short-wave radio communication with Benugan army commanders. Prime Minister Mr. Nwokedi convinced me that the junta's forces will carry out a genocide if they take Port Victoria. That city could fall in ten days unless we intervene.

(This upsets the Prime Minister.)

PRIME MINISTER: Now then, Hugh, steady on! We don't have the authority to intervene in the internal affairs of a sovereign nation. We can't just go barging in, can we? Britain isn't a colonial power any more, and we are a progressive socialist government.

SIR HUGH: Yes, but we created Bengara, Prime Minister! We maintain much of its educational and industrial infrastructure. We have leverage, surely?

PRIME MINISTER: We used to have "leverage," as you put it, but we now have competition on the international stage. Russia, China, the Gulf oil states... They are spreading their tentacles everywhere in our former colonies, and they want to replace us. My job is to hold on to what we've got! I can't antagonize the Muslim junta by overtly supporting the Bengugan Christians. As you pointed out, we have huge investments in Bengara, and I don't want to lose them.

SIR HUGH: Oh yes...and very soon, our biggest investment in Bengara will be oil... hundreds of millions of barrels waiting to be extracted...and all of it lies under the Christian enclave of Benugu. That's what this war is all about, isn't it?

(Silence)

PRIME MINISTER: We can't let the Russians get that oil. British oil companies found it, and they developed the roads to transport it to the ports. We have the rights to that oil, don't you see?

SIR HUGH: In this situation, Prime Minister, we have the moral duty to save millions of innocent lives. That takes precedence over our "oil rights."

PRIME MINISTER: "Moral duty?" You are the Foreign Secretary and a damn good one. I chose you because of your impeccable qualifications. You're a diplomat par excellence, so you, my friend, can afford to harbor noble ideals. Now, when you're in my position as the prime minister, you're in the front line-taking fire from all bloody sides! You have to face brutal facts. Now, here's a fact for you to consider. Strategically speaking, I have to prevent the Russians from controlling that oil-at all costs.

SIR HUGH: Even at the cost of becoming a party to genocide?

(Silence)

PRIME MINISTER: Now then, Hugh, you must know that I abhor the very thought of that monstrous crime! We've come up together, two working class boys from industrial cities in the North. We had to work and fight our way to political power. You know me as a friend...I am not going to facilitate a genocide; I'm going to go to the limits of my authority to prevent it... Try and appreciate my position. On top of everything else, I've got the Americans on my back. They're hell bent on keeping the Russians out because if they get the oil, they'll have the money to expand their nuclear program-and finance revolutions in the Third World!... And as we are the former colonial power in the region, the Americans expect me to bring a quick end to this war.

SIR HUGH: They do have a point. We are the established western power there, and it's our responsibility to avert mass murder. We have to act, Sir.

(Silence)

PRIME MINISTER: Act how? I would welcome any suggestions you have...

SIR HUGH: It's probably not what you want to hear... Give the Christian forces the means to stop and reverse the advance on Port Victoria. Give them what you gave the Muslim junta...heavy artillery. They also need anti-aircraft missiles to stop the Russian Migs from bombing and strafing them. If the junta have no air cover, they will have to retreat from Port Victoria... There'll be a stalemate, and that's what we need to bring both sides to the negotiating table.

PRIME MINISTER: Your idea of effecting a stalemate has merit. Matter of fact it has crossed my mind. The situation is dire, and we can't let it unravel into a catastrophe...Look, regarding the anti-aircraft missiles, if we were do anything, it would have to be covert. While I cannot directly supply them to the Benugans, I can give consideration to "unconventional" means...

SIR HUGH: I'm afraid I don't follow.

PRIME MINISTER: Being in a position of power sometimes necessitates cutting cards with the devil. I have had to deal with many devils on the international stage, Hugh. There's one who owes me a big favor. He has lots of anti-aircraft missiles, and conveniently, they're made in Germany. He may consider selling them to us...through an anonymous third party. If I can pull this off, the missiles could be flown to Port Victoria by rogue air freight companies. I can get MI-6 to organize the transfer.

SIR HUGH: Well, if your man cooperates, that will certainly even the odds for the Benugans. When will you know if this is feasible?

PRIME MINISTER: Leave that to me, Hugh. All I can tell you is that this fellow likes British pounds, and I'm prepared to offer him twenty million for the missiles...

SIR HUGH: Twenty million should be a powerful incentive for him to sell. Would I have come across this "individual," Prime Minister?

(Sir Hugh is suspicious)

**PRIME MINISTER
(laughs):**   I don't think so... He's a South American dictator of the worst sort, but he's an Anglophile. His daughter goes to Rodean. Amazing how these puffed-up foreign tyrants admire our public schools...

SIR HUGH: I see... Well, all I can say is, the very best of luck.

(Said with undisguised skepticism)

PRIME MINISTER: It's a long shot, but it's worth taking...I mean, we have to do something, eh? Look, I think it's time I met the antagonists in this conflict. I want to meet General bin Musa, the ambassador of Bangara. I'd like to persuade him to consider a negotiated settlement. I would also like to talk to the fellow from Benugu, Mister... No...

SIR HUGH: "Nwokedi."

PRIME MINISTER: "Nwokedi." Good, I want him to know, in the presence of General Musa that his views are important to me...to the British government. If we could get these two to communicate with each other in the spirit of mutual respect, they could influence their respective governments to start a peace process...

(Beat)

I actually care about his people, you know...and I cannot allow a genocide to a blemish my record!

SIR HUGE: Yes, Sir, history rarely overlooks a genocide, and having one on your record will certainly be detrimental to your European Union ambitions.

                         (The Prime Minister discerns the insult)

PRIME MINISTER: I make no apologies for having them! I am committed to a global government regulated by men and women of goodwill and reason. We have to elevate the human race above the greed and savagery of nationalist leaders...We must advance to the universal ideal of Tennyson. "The war drum throbbed no longer in the parliament of man, the Federation of the world..." That is the vision that must be realized-and in my time. If we had a global government, Foreign Secretary, this disastrous war in an obscure African country would never have happened!

ACT III, SCENE III.

A PRIVATE ROOM IN A POSH LONDON RESTAURANT. THE
PRIME MINISTER IS SITTING AT A TABLE WITH AVERY
FOREST, THE AMERICAN AMBASSADOR. HE IS AROUND
FIFTY, TALL AND GOOD LOOKING. HE IS SUITED BY
BROOKS BROTHERS. AVERY EXUDES THE CONFIDENCE OF
AN IVY LEAGUE ARISTOCRAT. A BOTTLE OF RED WINE IS
ON THE TABLE; THE PRIME MINISTER PICKS IT UP AND
POURS TWO GLASSES.

PRIME MINISTER: Thank you for consenting to this informal meeting, mister ambassador. I know you must be very involved with the situation in Iraq.

AVERY FOREST: That's for sure, Harry. Fighting an insurgency can be complicated. Iraq has become a hell hole, and the Russians are doing their best to magnify our problems.

(They pick up their glasses)

Cheers!

(They sip their wine)

...How about you? The European Union negotiations working out?

PRIME MINISTER: Well, I have to overcome opposition from certain Eastern European countries who resent the British-but. I do have the support of the major players.

AVERY FOREST: We would welcome a British president of the EU, Harry. I think you know that?

PRIME MINISTER: I appreciate the support, Avery... Europe needs Britain, both economically and militarily. I intend to do everything in my power to ensure our leadership role.

AVERY FOREST: I don't have to tell you that Europe has many faces...and most of them are insincere. I'll be happy to share any intelligence with you which could be useful.

PRIME MINISTER: Thank you...It's always good to be forewarned about who intends to shoot you in the back.

**AVERY FOREST
(laughs):**   You do have a way with words, Harry...How's Mary keeping?

PRIME MINISTER: She's doing well, thanks. Her painting is coming along nicely.

AVERY FOREST: I saw one of her landscapes the last time Nancy and I came over for dinner. I loved the one with the mist-shrouded hills...

PRIME MINISTER: Ah yes, that was Aviemore in Scotland.

AVERY FOREST: Beautiful...full of subtlety. It captured the spirit of the Highlands for me...So what's on your mind, Harry? You said it was urgent.

(Beat)

PRIME MINISTER: Avery, I'm caught up in a situation that both our countries are involved in.

AVERY FOREST: There are so many-which one?

PRIME MINISTER: The civil war in Bengara. You probably know that the Bengaran junta is about to eradicate the remnants of the rebel army in Port Victoria.

AVERY FOREST: Oh, you mean the Benugans. They're the Christian minority who want their own state. Apparently, they were persecuted forever by the Muslim majority tribes.

PRIME MINISTER: From what I know, after we handed over the reins of power, they were kept out of successive administrations by the Muslims. Naturally, the Muslims had a large majority in their parliament. They passed harsh laws against the Christians, and things came to a violent head when a coup was staged by Muslim army officers. All of them, unfortunately, were of the "radical" persuasion...they wanted total control in a new Islamic state.

AVERY FOREST: We're dealing with these damn fanatics in Iraq and Syria. This new form of an old religion is disturbing...it's violent, chaotic, and unpredictable.

PRIME MINISTER: The Muslim junta under General Amir Khan declared that all Christians were to be stripped of their civil rights and property. The Christians revolted and formed their own army in the Benugan enclave. Civil war then broke out, and General Amir Khan declared that he would exterminate the Christian population.in obedience to his religious duty

AVERY FOREST: As I understand it, he's well on the way to doing that... but the Benugan Christians are putting up one hell of a fight! I have to admire them Harry, but they're no match for the heavy artillery you supplied to General Khan...bad move.

PRIME MINISTER
(very apologetically):   You know, I...

AVERY FOREST
(cutting him off):   ...It's never good policy to give too much lethal hardware to these new African nations. They'll use it without the slightest regard for the niceties of war... So now, you have a major public relations problem. Britain can't afford to be implicated in a holocaust. That includes you...

                    (Silence)

PRIME MINISTER:

I have to concede that I made a huge mistake...I believed that the guns would bring a quick end to a bloody civil war. I'm trying to bring both sides to the negotiating table, Avery. A fanatical religion is certainly a great obstacle to reasoned mediation...but we both know what this war is really about, don't we?

AVERY FOREST
(laughs):

Oil... Oil! There's more oil in the Benugan enclave than there is in Saudi Arabia! And as you can appreciate, we have to get exclusive control over it. I'll give it to you straight, Harry...we can't allow the Russians, or any other power, to gain possession of it. So, we need you, as the former colonial power, to persuade the winning side in this war to give us their full cooperation...I think we both know which side will prevail? You're a stand-up guy, Harry...I know you'll get this done.

(Silence)

PRIME MINISTER:

To your point about the oil...about exclusivity...Avery, let me remind you that we founded Bengara. We created the infrastructure, the roads, and railways. A British company discovered the oil... We naturally expect to have the majority interest in the oil.

AVERY FOREST: What you're asking is who gets the lion's share...and you're asking the wrong guy. Come on, Harry, you're the Prime Minister of Great Britain. You must know that the oil giants control governments? You must know that the real decision makers are the CEOs of the international corporations and that they dictate policy?

PRIME MINISTER: I am aware that the oil lobby is the most powerful in Washington.

AVERY FOREST: And they will decide who shares the oil in foreign countries...and they tell the president how it will be. You should know the limits of "democracy" by now? It does what big business tells it to do.

PRIME MINISTER: Our oil companies have to get their share, Avery! They did the exploration; they've laid the transportation infrastructure to get the oil to port terminals!

AVERY FOREST: They'll get their cut, no problem...You see, Harry, all the oil companies are just one big happy, conniving family. There's a pecking order they all respect. They don't involve governments. They all recognize the eternal law of business: the big dogs get to eat first... That's the dynamic of capitalist prosperity, right?

(Beat)

PRIME MINISTER: Yes Avery, that's indisputable...and I do
know my place in the "pecking order..."
Thank you for being frank.

AVERY FOREST
(chuckles):   Just doing my job, Harry... Now we've
got all that over with. Why don't we get
together for another round of golf? I'll let
you beat me this time.

PRIME MINISTER: You're too kindhearted, Avery...it's
overwhelming me. Cheers!

ACT III, SCENE I.

OFFICE OF THE FOREIGN SECRETARY, SIR HUGH WINTHROP. HE IS ON HIS CELL PHONE (FLIP TOP), PACING AS HE TALKS.

SIR HUGH: Well, Prime Minister, perhaps it wasn't a good idea to talk to the American ambassador... Of course, they don't want to get their hands dirty...they don't want any involvement... We're their "fall guys" in this mess!

(He walks listens)

...So, when are we meeting with General Musa today? At four?

I'll have to cancel a reception at the Indian embassy...it's for some sitar player, very popular over here too...All right, at four, then... Fine, I'll be there with James and Mr. Nwokedi...We're taking a big risk putting him together with General Musa...I really think... Damn! Damn! He's cut me off again! Impossible man!

(He pockets the phone and walks to his desk. He picks up a newspaper and reads it briefly, frowning with concern. James Donald enters.)

JAMES DONALD: Good morning, Sir Hugh.

SIR HUGH: Any news?

JAMES DONALD: About Benugu? No. I'll be in touch with Mr. Nwokedi later. He may have received an update from Port Victoria by radio.

SIR HUGH: Well, you can give him this update: his presence is requested by the Prime Minister at 10 Downing Street at four this afternoon. He'll be meeting another guest, General Musa...

JAMES DONALD: Well, what could possibly go wrong? I hope they're placed at opposite ends of the conference table. Bin Musa is prone to violent behavior.

SIR HUGH: I'm sure the Prime Minister is aware of that possibility. I don't think General Musa will misbehave in Number 10... He respects power, and he knows that the Prime Minister has plenty of it.

JAMES DONALD: I'm sure he's aware that we still supply the junta with artillery...

**SIR HUGH
(interrupts):**   ...and guns are useless without the ammunition that we're still providing. That's part of the disastrous agreement the Prime Minister made with the junta.

JAMES DONALD: This whole thing is deranged... Do you think the Prime Minister knows what he is doing any more? He's ignored sound advice, especially from you, and he's mired us in a humanitarian disaster. Doesn't he realize that if we don't prevent a genocide, he'll bear much of the responsibility for creating it?

SIR JAMES: I spoke to him at length yesterday. He's painfully aware of the immense damage it can cause to his political career...especially to his European Union aspirations. He thinks he can affect a stalemate by persuading some unnamed South American dictator to supply the Christian forces with German anti-aircraft missiles...

JAMES DONALD: I'm even more convinced now that he is in urgent need of psychiatric care. He's delusional!

SIR HUGH: Of course, it's just wishful thinking on his part, James... Nothing will come of it...It sems inevitable that those Russian planes will bomb Port Victoria to rubble...and the population will be wiped out...

JAMES DONALD: And when that happens, the world will see that we have blood on our hands, and it will never wash off.

ACT III, SCENE III.

A RECEPTION ROOM IN LAMBETH PALACE, THE RESIDENCE OF THE ARCHBISHOP OF CANTERBURY, FELICITY GORDON-WALKER. THE PRIME MINISTER WAITS FOR HER, PASSING THE TIME BY LOOKING AT THE PORTRAITS OF PAST ARCHBISHOPS WHICH DECORATE THE WALLS. THE ENTRANCE DOOR IS UPSTAGE/LEFT. THE ARCHBISHOP AND THE PRIME MINISTER WERE FRIENDS AT CAMBRIDGE. SHE ENTERS THE ROOM. SHE IS WIRY, OF MEDIUM HEIGHT, HER HAIR CROPPED VERY SHORT. SHE WEARS BLACK SLACKS AND A WHITE POLO-NECKED SWEATER. HER MANNER IS EFFUSIVE, FRENETIC.

ARCHBISHOP
(gushing): Oh Harry, how nice of you to come and see me! Sorry, Lambeth Palace is in such a mess...we're going through yet another refurbishment. My you've put on weight; you must have a super chef at Number 10!

PRIME MINISTER: Well, he did train in Paris, and...

ARCHBISHOP
(CUTTING HIM OFF): I thought so! Probably a full-blown cordon bleu, you lucky devil! How's your beautiful Mary keeping?

PRIME MINISTER: Couldn't be better, Felicity. She finally passed her driving test.

ARCHBISHOP: Oh, how fantastic! I got mine after graduating from Cambridge, but I hardly do any driving now. One of the advantages of being the Archbishop of Canterbury is that I get driven all over the place by an amazing chauffeur,

PRIME MINISTER: An ex-policeman, I suppose?

ARCHBISHOP (Chuckles): Actually, no, he's a defrocked vicar who had an affair with his housekeeper's daughter-she was underage, but only by a year, though...

PRIME MINISTER: Is it wise to engage someone...

ARCHBISHOP: Oh, he's really such a sweet fellow! We're "rehabbing" him. Trusting him is so essential to his full recovery. We mustn't be judgmental, must we?

PRIME MINISTER: No, no, of course not...that wouldn't be very Christian, would it?

ARCHBISHOP: Of course not! Christ did not come to judge but to forgive. My mission, as the head of the Anglican faith community, is to create a world of love and forgiveness. Love is the very heart of all religions, isn't it?

PRIME MINISTER: I'd like to believe that, Felicity, but religion has been the cause of horrendous wars, intolerance. And genocidal hatred.

ARCHBISHOP: Yes, but that's the old religion, Harry...We now have advanced into the new enlightenment, a religion which is universal, respecting all life, promoting non-judgmental tolerance and understanding. We who guide our churches realize that we are all equal that no one religion is superior to the others. After all, we share the same "god," don't we? A god of sublime love and peace.

(Silence.)

PRIME MINISTER: I do admire your passionate conviction, Felicity. I am well aware of your interfaith programs, particularly your highly publicized outreach to the Muslim leaders of our country.

ARCHBISHOP: Oh, it's been wildly successful, Harry! The Muslims are so welcoming when I speak in their mosques. I love Islam...it's such a noble and peaceful religion, don't you think? We collaborate with many wonderful Muslim charities here in London. They do great work with the homeless.

PRIME MINISTER: I presume then that you, as the Archbishop of Canterbury, are on excellent terms with the leading Imams in the Muslim communities.

ARCHBISHOP: Of course! Especially with the Grand Imam of London, he's such a darling...He's loved and respected all over the world-the Pope has invited him to the Vatican many times. You know, I love going to his mosque for the Iftar dinner every year... Needless to say my partner Pam and I have hosted the Grand Imam here in Lambeth Palace. He loves English food-as long as it's halal, of course.

(she chortles stupidly)

PRIME MINISTER: I'm glad that you've established such cordial relations with the Muslim community, Felicity. You see, your friendship with the Grand Imam could be of great service in saving thousands of lives.

(Beat)

ARCHBISHOP: Oh, my goodness. Well, I'll do whatever I can, Harry. What's this about?

PRIME MINISTER: You must be aware of the civil war in Bengara?

ARCHBISHOP: Oh yes. It's tribal, isn't it? From what I've been hearing from my people there, it will blow over soon. I seem to recall a news item on the BBC. Something about Port Victoria being in difficulties...

PRIME MINISTER: Port Victoria is under siege by a Muslim army that will destroy it, along with its population of three million Christians. There will be a genocide unless we find a way to stop it.

(Silence)

ARCHBISHOP: Oh my God! This is horrific...so distressing! You say a Muslim army? I don't understand... What could have provoked them to such violence? Did the Christians attack them first?

PRIME MINISTER: No, there was a coup initiated by senior Muslim officers in the Bengaran army. They were united in their belief in the supremacy of Islam over all other religions. They wanted the whole of Bengara to be a Muslim theocracy under sharia law. The Christians in the Benugu enclave refused to comply with their demand to submit to Islam. Their resistance was met with repression and massacres.

(Beat)

ARCHBISHOP: This is ghastly...outrageous! These Muslim officers are hijacking Islam! This is a hideous desecration of Islamic teaching. Islam is an Abrahamic faith and it shares our values and principles.

PRIME MINISTER: Be that as it may, Muslim soldiers attacked Christians living in Muslim majority areas, forcing them to seek refuge in Benugu-the Christian enclave. The Christian forces were outnumbered and... outgunned... They retreated to their last stronghold in Port Victoria... The city will fall in a few days, and a genocide will ensue....

ARCHBISHOP: Well, for heaven's sake, Harry! You're the Prime Minister, why haven't you done something to stop this?

PRIME MINISTER: I can't, Felicity...things have changed since our days at Cambridge. We're not a world empire any more. I can't use force, but I can use persuasion...that's why I need your help. Your friendship with the Grand Imam could turn things around...you could be a catalyst for peace.

(Silence)

ARCHBISHOP: I won't abuse my friendship with the Grand Imam, Harry. You and I have been friends for decades, but I can't compromise the trust I've built with the leader of the Muslim community.

PRIME MINISTER: I'm not asking you to compromise that friendship, Felicity... In fact, I'm sure that the Grand Imam will approve of your effort to save thousands of innocent lives...

ARCHBISHOP: He's a man of great compassion. Go on...

PRIME MINISTER: I need you to support me in a meeting tomorrow with the Bengaran ambassador, General Musa. He's a powerful member of the Muslim Junta that is intent on eradicating the Christians. If you can convince him that, as you say, Islam is a religion of peace, of compassion...you can make him reconsider his government's policy.... I'm hoping that you and your "god" will prevail...

ACT III, SCENE III.

A CONFERENCE ROOM IN 10 DOWNING STREET. PRESENT ARE: HARRY CROSSMAN, THE PRIME MINISTER, THE FOREIGN SECRETARY, SIR HUGH WINTHROP, JAMES DONALD, HIS AIDE, TONY NWOKEDI, THE REPRESENTATIVE OF BENUGU; GENERAL MUSA, THE AMBASSADOR OF BENGARA; FELICITY GORDON PARKER, THE ARCHBISHOP OF CANTERBURY, AND WILLIAM BUTLER, THE CEO OF INTERNATIONAL OIL AND GAS ASSOCIATES.

ALL FACE THE AUDIENCE BEHIND A LONG TABLE. THE PRIME MINISTER IS IN THE MIDDLE. TO HIS S/LEFT IS HIS AIDE, JAMES DONALD. TO HIS S/R IS SIR HUGH. TO THE S/L OF JAMES DONALD IS THE ARCHBISHOP. TO THE S/R OF SIR HUGH IS TONY NWOKEDI. TO THE S/L OF THE ARCHBISHOP IS GENERAL BIN MUSA. TO THE S/R OF TONY NWOKEDI IS WILLIAM BUTLER.

THE PRIME MINISTER STANDS.

PRIME MINISTER: Thank you all for being here. First, allow me to make the necessary introductions....

(he points to the people he names)

...Sir Hugh Winthrop, the Foreign Secretary, his aide, Mr. Donald. Mr. Tony Nwokedi, the representative of Benugu... General Musa, the ambassador of Bengara. We have all had separate discussions on the matter at hand. I want to cordially welcome my old university friend, Felicity Gordon-Walker, the Archbishop of Canterbury...

ARCHBISHOP
(interrupts): ...thank you so much, Prime Minister, I'm so looking forward to serving the cause of peace in Bengara!

PRIME MINISTER: You grace us with your presence, Archbishop. Sitting on your left is General Musa, the ambassador of Bengara. General, I can say that the archbishop is a great admirer of your religion.

ARCHBISHOP
(gushing): You may have heard of my interfaith outreach programs, General? The BBC did a whole documentary on them. Did you see it?

GENERAL MUSA: No, madam, the trash on the BBC doesn't interest me.

ARCHBISHOP
(flustered):   Oh, oh, I'm sorry, general... The Grand Imam of London was featured in it, you know.

GENERAL MUSA: That comes as no surprise, he craves publicity. (He addresses the Prime Minister) ...Can we move forward with this meeting, Prime Minister? I hate wasting my time.

                              (The PM, James Donald, Tony Nwokedi, and Sir Hugh are appalled by his rudeness)

PRIME MINISTER: Yes, General, and time is of the essence... But before I start, I need to make one more introduction... Mr. William Butler, the CEO of the International Oil Consortium. He is here at the invitation of General Musa. We welcome him as an expert on the crucial significance of the oil industry in this situation. Mr. Butler, a few words, please?

WILLIAM BUTLER: Thank you kindly, Prime Minister. I hope to give you all an accurate and comprehensive view of the goals of my industry. We're as anxious as you are to arrive at a resolution to the civil war in Bengara. I am grateful for the opportunity to participate here.

PRIME MINISTER: Thank you for accepting, Mr. Butler... All right then, let's get down to business... We are here to face our responsibilities as leaders in our respective spheres of influence. We're here to prevent a human catastrophe...We are all aware of the impending assault on Port Victoria in the Christian enclave of Benugu.

**GENERAL MUSA
(shouts):**   Objection! There was never a "Christian" enclave! Call it by its proper name, a "rebel enclave." They are all refuse, traitors!"

PRIME MINISTER: General bin Musa, we do recognize your government's position. What we have to do is find a way to prevent the killing of innocent civilians in Port Victoria!

**GENERAL MUSA
(snorts):**   They are not innocent! These rebels deserve no mercy! They've been killing the Muslims in Bengura. They double-crossed us!

TONY NWOKEDI: With respect, General bin Musa, your Muslim colleagues in the junta forced us to take up arms-in self-defense. Your soldiers stormed Christian villages, looting, raping, and murdering...They had embarked on a genocidal campaign to wipe out the Christian population... You should know because you commanded a brigade.

GENERAL MUSA: Yes, I did! And I am proud of our victories...

TONY NWOKEDI: Murdering defenseless women and children...

GENERAL MUSA: I make no apologies for eliminating Christian enemies who rebelled against our legitimate authority

TONY NWOKEDI: "Enemies? Unarmed pregnant women, your men eviscerated, young girls they publicly raped to death, chaining them to posts in the ground.

ARCHBISHOP: (SCREAMS) God! God! Stop! Stop!

(Nwokedi ignores her)

TONY NWOKEDI: Whole villages burned out, their populations herded into churches and incinerated!

ARCHBISHOP: For God's sake, I beg you, stop...Just stop...

(They keep silent)

...We have to look to solutions, not to recriminations...

TONY NWOKEDI: We can't look away from crimes against humanity, Archbishop.

GENERAL MUSA: Crimes? In my opinion, Archbishop, by eliminating those traitors, we did humanity a favor.

TONY NWOKEDI: You vile bastard!

(He jumps to his feet and makes a move towards General Musa. James Donald restrains him)

JAMES DONALD: Mr. Nwokedi, I know it's hard, but please let it go. We must not descend into violence here...Let's commit to being reasonable...in spite of provocations... Please, Mr. Nwokedi...

(He sits)

TONY NWOKEDI: I apologize...I've lost my parents and most of my relatives in the fighting...As you know, I'm facing the loss of my entire people.

(Silence)

ARCHBISHOP: My heart goes out to your people, Mr. Nwokedi, and it goes out to you, General Musa. I'm sure, too, have lost loved ones in this war?

GENERAL MUSA: One of the reasons for my determination to attain a final victory Archbishop.

PRIME MINISTER: General Musa, Mr. Nwokedi, we are aware of your pain and your differences...we're here to resolve them. We need to come together to save millions of innocent people. We're here to make a pathway to peace... Peace...that's why I invited my friend Felicity to be here. She's a healer of wounds.

ARCHBISHOP: Oh, Prime Minister, your praise is appreciated but not deserved. I just do what I can to enhance understanding and community cohesion.

JAMES DONALD: Honor where it is due, Archbishop... Your efforts have been invaluable.

PRIME MINISTER: The archbishop is a moderator who has united peoples of many different faiths, notably Islam and Christianity. Archbishop Gordon-Parker is respected by the Muslim leaders of Britain and enjoys the friendship of the Grand Imam of London...

(He turns to General Musa)

...my hope, General, is that she will make a friend of you.

(Beat. General Musa breaks out into a belly laugh)

GENERAL MUSA: Too kind, too kind, Prime Minister...Thank you!

Thank you so much...

(He stops laughing)

But, as a good Muslim, I have to choose my friends carefully.

(Beat)

And besides, anything else-she's not my type!

SIR HUGH
(angry):   Now look here, is there any need for this rudeness?

JAMES DONALD: It really isn't on, General!

ARCHBISHOP: General Musa, you wouldn't want me anyway because I'm a lesbian...I hope I don't offend you?

GENERAL MUSA: Franky madam, I find your kind repulsive.

PRIME MINISTER
(shouting):   General, can't we keep a civil tone here?

ARCHBISHOP: Prime Minister, I really appreciate the General's candor....

(She looks at the General)

...General, I regard your opinion of me as a starting point in our relationship. When I began my outreach to Islam, many of your co-religionists rejected me. Some of them even showed me the door. But I saw something in them that encouraged me. their honesty! They were unafraid to offend me, and I found that so very refreshing. When they saw that I respected their religious views, they allowed me to share mine.

GENERAL MUSA: And in my opinion, they were weak and foolish.

ARCHBISHOP
(gushing goodwill):   General Musa, Islam is a beautiful and peaceful religion, and I have been working tirelessly to nurture it in Britain. Your faith has been an invaluable addition to the multicultural diversity which now defines our nation.

(General Musa chuckles)

GENERAL MUSA: Madam, if you believe that Islam is a religion of peace, you are delusional...Islam's founder, the prophet Mohammed, peace be upon him, was a warrior, a warlord. He led military campaigns and killed thousands of Christians, Jews, and pagans, and other filthy infidels. He beheaded hundreds of his enemies, especially the Jews of Khybar...He made their women the sex slaves of his warriors and kept the best for himself...He was a conqueror sent by Allah to make Islam dominant in the earth.

ARCHBISHOP
(still gushing):   Yes, of course, Mohammed was divinely ordained! He was a great man! But when the fighting was over, he was kind and generous, wasn't he? He set such a good example that millions of people all over the world wanted to follow him.

GENERAL MUSA: If that is what your Imams are teaching you, then they have succeeded in making you a mindless propagandist- a useful idiot. Read the Koran for yourself!

PRIME MINISTER: General Musa, you need to show respect for the spiritual Head of the Anglican Church!

GENERAL MUSA: I am respecting her-by telling the truth! (Beat)

ARCHBISHOP: General Musa, I have been taking classes in Islam at the Grand Mosque in London. If you don't respect me, then you will respect my friend, the Grand Imam. His religion is one of mercy and tolerance. In fact, he has instructed me to tell you that if a Muslim kills just one man, it's like killing all men. Islam and Allah are merciful...

GENERAL MUSA
(in a civil tone now):   Archbishop, allow me to enlighten you...
That ruling applies only to a Muslim man
killing another Muslim man... We're not
allowed to do that, but we are allowed to
kill infidels. Here's the core teaching of the
Koran, Sura 2, verse 191: "Kill the infidel
wherever you find them..." This is
amplified in Sura 8:39:"...and slay the
infidel until they submit, and the only
religion on earth is Islam..." And I would be
remiss in not mentioning Sura 48:29..." Be
merciful to one another, but ruthless to the
infidel." And that is my Islam, and it is the
only Islam, my dear Archbishop. Islam will
conquer all the infidels in this planet,
including you...and when all of you become
good Muslims, there will be peace on earth,
an Islamic peace shared by Muslims alone.
Do you understand now?

(She reacts with unexpected anger)

ARCHBISHOP: What a horrifying vision of the future! It's
murderous, totally intolerant, and divisive!
It is hateful, and I find it revolting! You and
your junta are distorting and abusing a great
world religion! You've made it barbaric!

(Beat)

SIR HUGH: General Musa, I think we should focus on what can be done. We can't change religious beliefs held over centuries, but we can deal with the practical issues we are facing in Benugu-like saving thousands of innocent lives.

GENERAL MUSA: My religion is an important "practical" issue...but you don't want to face up to it. And that, Foreign Secretary, is your misfortune.

(Silence)

**PRIME MINISTER
(upbeat):**   What if your president, General Amir Khan, were given an "incentive" to halt the offensive? What if we could come up with an offer which he'll find very attractive? You, of course, will present it to him.

GENERAL MUSA: Let me make it very clear that the offer has to appeal to me- or I'll ignore it.

PRIME MINISTER: What sort of incentive would you be in favor of, General?

**GENERAL MUSA
(chuckles):**   What about a hundred million pounds, which I will administer as the Bengaran ambassador- and a member of the ruling junta? (Short silence. The Prime Minister turns to Sir Hugh)

PRIME MINISTER: What do you think, Sir Hugh?

SIR HUGH: Well, it could be arranged, Prime Minister. Of course, it would have to be spread over...let's say, five years.

JAMES DONALD: I think it will take at least a month to get parliamentary approval and the go-ahead from the Treasury. They're sticklers about how the money will be spent... We'll need specific projects, like building a dam or a reforestation program.

PRIME MINISTER: Yes, we'll need guarantees to that effect, General.

GENERAL MUSA: I can tell you now that my president will not approve. He wants hard cash in a Swiss banking account-with no strings attached.

PRIME MINISTER: I'm afraid that can't be done...We can't just transfer a hundred million pounds into a Swiss banking account! Parliament would never approve of it.

GENERAL MUSA: Then forget about your "incentive," Prime Minister:

JAMES DONALD: Look, General Musa, there's got to be something your president wants...more than committing a genocide...

GENERAL MUSA: What he wants, and this is non-negotiable, is to eradicate any opposition to the Islamic state we have been fighting for. What he wants is the total annihilation of the Christian rebels in Benugu. We are very close to it now, and you cannot stop us! You call it a genocide, but we call it a glorious victory for Allah.

PRIME MINISTER (explodes): Man, have you no compassion for the innocents your soldiers will murder? Your callous and inflexible stance is abhorrent! You are forcing me to adopt extraordinary measures because I will not...I will not have a genocide to mar my record as Prime Minister of Great Britain!

GENERAL MUSA: Your record is the least of our considerations, and it's too late to save it...We succeeded with the artillery you supplied us, Prime Minister... This is on you. (The Prime Minister is in dread at this truth)

PRIME MINISTER: It's not too late...I can meet with your president, and I will give him an ultimatum... If the attack on Port Victoria is not called off, all aid...all aid to Bengara will be cut off...immediately! I will also tell him that you took it upon yourself to turn down an offer of a hundred million pounds in an aid package. Your president and Junta won't be pleased to hear that, will they?

GENERAL MUSA: All right, cards on the table! My president has other aid flowing in, which makes your offer insignificant! I threw out that demand for a hundred million pounds just to test and annoy you...You know what would have happened to that money if we received it? The president and the junta would have enjoyed it-without giving you anything in return...

(He chuckles)

So, you see, your former subjects are now duping you for a change. Keep your damn money; we have more than we need to complete our assault on Port Victoria.

(The Prime Minister panics)

PRIME MINISTER: All right, I'll exercise my power, under international humanitarian law, to use force to crush your advance on Port Victoria! We can bomb your forward positions. I'll order the destruction of your airfields and those Russian fighters! I'll deploy our crack commando units to create havoc behind your lines...

(Silence)

GENERAL MUSA: Said like a politician who is desperate to
                           protect his record. Sorry, but I can't help
                           you. You are powerless to make a move.
                           You would be upsetting your masters in the
                           United States and the international oil
                           companies who pay them handsomely for
                           their... "cooperation." They want this war to
                           be over soon because they can't wait to
                           exploit our oil fields in Benugu. We've
                           made a deal with them, Prime Minister, and
                           they won't allow you to break it.

                           (The Prime Minister knows that he is
                           helpless)

PRIME MINISTER: I don't believe you have a deal... Saving the
                           lives of thousands of innocent people will
                           be more important to the United States than
                           your oil... Britain and the United States are
                           principled nations... We don't sanction
                           genocide.

GENERAL MUSA: You are out of your depth, unaware of all
                           the forces at play here. With idiots like you
                           in charge, it's is no wonder that the British
                           Empire collapsed into obscurity. (Sir Hugh
                           tries to deflect bin Musa's attack on the
                           Prime Minister)

SIR HUGH: I beg to differ, General. We are the sixth-largest economy in the world, and our armed forces may be small, but they're lethal. Hitler, to his chagrin, scoffed at the warning Hermann Goering gave him at the beginning of the war: "Never underestimate the British..." Public opinion is the most important weapon we have, and the British public will be enraged when they hear of your plan to commit genocide! Contrary to what you think, they will approve of a military intervention to save the Christians of Benugu.

GENERAL MUSA: How can an intelligent man like you believe that? The British public has grown too bloated and complacent to care about people dying in some obscure African country. The British people have become enslaved by pleasure, by the "good" life. They are possessed by the godless luxuries of your thriving economy... Oh yes, they will be impressed by the impassioned editorials which will compare the junta to the Nazi Party, but the furor will die down in a few days...Some duchess will fall off her horse and break her leg, or some bishop will be found screwing an altar boy, or some debauched rock star will die of a drug overdose... These fruits of your degeneracy will fill the minds of your great British public...not a genocide in Africa.

(Silence. There is an awareness of the truth in what the general says)

JAMES DONALD: I wouldn't be so sure, general bin Musa. The British were thought to be degenerate before, and Hitler described our young men as being useless and effete... They proved him wrong. It's never advisable to put us to the test, and it proved fatal to the Nazis. We fight best when our backs are pushed against the wall...I strongly advise you not to do that.

GENERAL MUSA: Mr. Donald, your backs are up against the wall, but I am not the one doing the pushing. I think this is the time for Mr. William Butler to give us his opinion...I believe that his expertise will be enlightening...and of crucial importance to this meeting. Mr. Butler, would you please acquaint us with the realities of the situation? (Butler speaks in a measured, confident way, totally dispassionate).

WILLIAM BUTLER: Madam Archbishop, Prime Minister Crossman, gentlemen... My company is worth over two trillion dollars. We are the most successful company in the international oil business. We help countries develop their oil and mineral resources and make them commercially viable. We don't waste their time, and we get results. Over 50 nations like to do business with us because we create prosperity, a necessity for political stability.

PRIME MINISTER: Mr. Butler, we are well aware of your company's influence, and we acknowledge your contribution too many of our former colonies. Now, with regard to Bengara and its Christian enclave of Benugu, we have an immense problem. There's a civil war which has almost come to its conclusion-a genocide. We have to stop it.

WILLIAM BUTLER: I totally agree... My company has acquired the exclusive rights to the oilfields in the Benugu enclave...I know this comes as a surprise to you, but we don't disclose our acquisitions until we have to...I guess this is the time for you to know.

(Silence. The PM and everyone else is shocked)

PRIME MINISTER: I would have thought that, as the former colonial power, you would have informed us earlier.

SIR HUGH: That's a common courtesy, wouldn't you say?

WILLIAM BUTLER: We were under no legal obligation, Foreign Secretary... but I am here to assure you that International Oil and Mineral Resources want an end to hostilities as soon as possible. I'll be upfront with you. I have to inform you that my company has tried, since the war started a year ago, to persuade the leaders of the Christian enclave to surrender...We looked at their situation and concluded that it was a lost cause. We therefore guaranteed them safe passage to a third country, with generous financial compensation. Unfortunately, they refused.

TONY NWOKEDI: Butler, no such offer was made! You are lying! You made a deal with the Muslim junta to get exclusivity to our oil by giving them billions to purchase weapons. Your dirty money has made it possible for them to buy the Russian fighters, which forced our retreat. You have facilitated a war crime against my people!

WILLIAM BUTLER: Come now, Sir! I think we need to be fair here. If anyone is responsible for the victories of the Muslim armies, it's the British government! They knew all along that the Christian militias had no defense against heavy artillery...but they went ahead a supplied them. You also sent a few military advisors, didn't you, Prime Minister?

                         (Silence.)

PRIME MINISTER
(subdued)   It has always been our policy to supply our former colonies with the necessary arms for their defense. As for the artillery...I had no idea it would be used...with such devastating effect...

                         (Sir Hugh is infuriated at the lie)

SIR HUGH: Well Prime Minister, I did make the information available to you. I did my job in sharing that intelligence. I gave you the assessment of our military attaché in Owerra, the capital. We didn't have to send those guns!

PRIME MINISTER: You gave me those assessments after...after I agreed to supply the weapons to the junta! I didn't know how ghastly and vicious this war would become. I believed it was a tribal clash which would be followed by a quick victory…for the junta. It was inevitable, wasn't it?

(He sounds slightly hysterical)

TONY NWOKEDI: No, Prime Minister, it was not inevitable. You misjudged the courage and determination of my people. You imagined that after being pounded by your guns that, they would fold and surrender. But we kept retreating and resisting the barbarians... and now we've got our backs to the sea. We have lost over a half a million people, and you have their blood on your hands... You're trying to assuage your conscience now by your vain attempt to stop the final assault. You're trying to cover up your monumental mistake... You knew what you were doing when you sent those guns. You knew the consequences... You are a hypocrite!

(General Musa laughs)

GENERAL MUSA: Nwokedi, life is full of surprises... You and I are in perfect agreement on this... He is a monumental hypocrite... (He turns to the archbishop and continues) ...It's such a pity that your Christians in Benugu put their faith in them because these people are no longer Christian.

ARCHBISHOP: What an awful thing to say! We Christians are living our faith by trying to save lives! That's our duty. Your criticism of the Prime Minister is not deserved. I have known him since our university days, and he is a man of integrity. He did not intend this disaster to happen.

PRIME MINISTER: I didn't know what the situation was on the ground...I was trying to bring an end to the conflict... One side had to win, didn't it? The Muslims outnumbered the Christians by six-to-one...they had no chance of winning.

TONY NWOKEDI: You backed the side that openly advocates the killing of all non-Muslims. The side that hates Judeo-Christian civilization, which you brought to Africa. We in Benugu welcomed you. We shared a kinship of values with you when we converted to Christianity. We respected you, and yes, we loved you. And you, Prime Minister, betrayed the Christian pastors who came to us...you nullified their sacrifice.

(The Prime Minister is remorseful but not cowed)

PRIME MINISTER: All I can do, Mr. Nwokedi, is apologize...I made a mistake, I take responsibility for that...I had no idea that I was dealing with religious fanatics.

(Beat)

WILLIAM BUTLER: Gentlemen, apologies and recriminations won't serve our purpose. We're wasting time, and mine has a high value. The way I see it, we are at an impasse. In Bengara, we have a fight to the death... The Muslims want to exterminate the Christians, and the Christians will fight to the last man. It's a no-win situation. We all tried, in our own ways, to affect a resolution. Mr. Nwokedi just accused me of promoting a genocide, ignoring my efforts to transport the entire Christian population to safety. My company was chartering ocean liners to do that!

TONY NWOKEDI: I have no way of knowing that this is true. You're making yourself out to be a humanitarian now, a savior of my people... Tell me this, when the rapists and murderers have annihilated my people, will you still do business with them?

(Silence)

WILLIAM BUTLER
(unruffled):

If we don't act on agreements made with the junta, which were signed long before the dire situation in Port Victoria, the Russians will step right in. Maybe the Chinese too... You wouldn't want that to happen, would you, Prime Minister? That would be a huge setback for the Commonwealth, right?

(He chuckles)

You know, the trouble with you guys in Britain is that you don't have the guts to face harsh realities....to harness the new political forces that have formed in this world. You try to pretend that they don't exist.

TONY NWOKEDI:

Does that include the people who flew jets into the Twin Towers, killing over three thousand Americans? The people who worship a god who extolls mass rape, genocidal murder, and beheadings? Will you do business with this "new political force?"

WILLIAM BUTLER: I face the facts; however unpalatable they may be...I am aware of what the Muslim forces are doing in Benugu. Their savagery is a given in this equation...but it is better to engage with them than not to.

(He lightens up)

Surely you know the old Russian adage that it is wise to hug your enemy close? That way, he can't lift a hand to knife you in the back. We are not afraid to make deals with whose beliefs abhorrent to our own. We get what we need from them, and we keep them happy with what everybody on earth wants.... the American dollar! Business has to deal with the winning side in any war, and sadly, Mr. Nwokedi, your side lost.

TONY NWOKEDI: And the world loses too, Mr. Butler... Eventually, you and your kind will destroy it because you have no humanity...no love of honor... You value your profit margins above justice and freedom. My people are an inconvenience to your global plans and so...they are expendable. But your billions won't wash our blood off your hands....

WILLIAM BUTLER: Well, I am done here... Mr. Nwokedi, I have to work with what I cannot change...

(He rises)

Prime Minister Crossman, Madam Archbishop. Gentlemen, I hope you can resolve what I couldn't.

(He walks out. Silence)

ARCHBISHOP: Prime Minister, we need to take extraordinary measures; we're at the eleventh hour. I propose that I fly out to Bengara to meet with General Amir Khan. I will beg him to call a ceasefire.

GENERAL MUSA: I don't see the point, Archbishop...We who follow the true Islam don't talk to women; we keep them in the kitchen and the bedroom. To make matters worse, you are a lesbian, and you, therefore, qualify for the death penalty.

TONY NWOKEDI: He's right, Archbishop...In General Musa's Islam, women are the property of men. They are forbidden to have a voice in the governance of their nations...prohibited from talking on equal terms with leaders like General Khan... He'll just insult and degrade you and put you on a plane back to Britain-if you're lucky.

ARCHBISHOP:	But surely, he would respect my office? Look past my natural sexual preference, which was God-given? Surely, he would respect my leadership of sixty million people all over the world?
GENERAL MUSA:	That is what makes you a high-value target, Archbishop. Can't you understand? You are the enemy...

(Silence. The archbishop is hurt confused)

ARCHBISHOP:	Well...so far as I am concerned, I don't have any enemies...only people I can win over as friends. My religion does not put people into mutually exclusive categories. It does not brand them as "good" or "evil..." It does not classify them as being "right" or "wrong." General Musa, can't you see that your kind of Islam condemns humanity to an eternal religious war?
GENERAL MUSA:	Eternal war...if that is what Allah wants, then so be it... We will establish the Dar al Islam, the world of Islam, in which there will be no Jews, no Christians, no Hindus and Buddhists... only Muslims. We Muslims are commanded by the Koran to conquer you...as we shall conquer our Christian enemies in Port Victoria... Killing in the name of Allah is our sacred duty.

TONY NWOKEDI: We won't make it easy for you, General. Street fighting in a city is the nightmare of every commander. We'll fight to the last man, and I plan of being there for the end.

GENERAL MUSA: Good show, Nwokedi, I must admire your spirit-futile, though it is. I respect your loyalty to your people. The only way they can survive is to convert to Islam, and I can't see that happening...

(He rises)

Well, I see no point in continuing this discussion. I have a dinner engagement at six and must hurry. She hates being kept waiting. Goodbye.

(He walks out)

JAMES DONALD: Mr. Nwokedi, I urge you not to return to Benugu. The odds are that you will be killed...Your people will need a leader of your caliber after the war. There will be survivors, and you could be of immense help to them....

TONY NWOKEDI: Mr. Donald, living in Britain is no longer a valid choice for me. This country has lost its moral integrity, and I no longer belong here. It's not a Christian country any longer.

SIR HUGH:

Mr. Nwokedi a man of your honor and moral stature is crucially important to the Benugan Christians. I can think of no better man to   speak for them. You can be the hope for their future. I beg you to reconsider.

(Nwokedi is touched by the tributes)

TONY NWOKEDI:

Thank you, Sir Hugh.... Mr. Donald... You know, you are in danger of extinction too. You are both the remnants of the Britain I loved. I hope you will survive the descent into degeneracy.

JAMES DONALD:

I think the Foreign Secretary and I are aware of the sullied world we live in... It is far from perfect, full of liars, thieves, destroyers of the innocent, traitors to what we revered and lived for. I too feel betrayed, but I have faith in the values that made us great: honesty courage, decency... These values are eternal, and no force can kill them.

TONY NWOKEDI:

You put it very well, Mr. Donald. Yes, they are eternal, and I know that they will once again prevail in the hearts of men...But we'll have to wait for Christ to return for that to happen.

ARCHBISHOP
(effusive):

But we don't have to wait! We can be Christ; we have to act like Christ; we have to carry the standard of Christ!

TONY NWOKEDI: Archbishop, if you carry the standard of Jesus Christ, it is devoid of his cross...Without it, you don't have any legitimacy as a Christian church. Frankly, I don't know what you believe in.

ARCHBISHOP: All right! I believe in a new world where old hatreds are buried in compassion, in the loving acceptance of differences... My God, Mr. Nwokedi, is the God of all, and therefore, all religions are pathways to him- and are of equal value. I live my Christianity, and I don't think of it as being superior to other faiths!

(Silence. Nwokedi smiles at her, incredulous)

TONY NWOKEDI: You know, Archbishop, the reason why primitive peoples in Africa believed in Christianity was because the priests and pastors proclaimed that it was indeed superior. Superior to their animist gods who had for so long kept them in ignorance, disease, and delusions. Christianity gave them the light of hope, of eternal salvation...And now, my people cannot look to you for guidance because you no longer believe that Christ is the way, the truth, and the light. You have surrendered his truth to an asinine, no-fault world religion. You and all your fellow "Christian" leaders are blind guides.

SIR HUGH: Not all of us have surrendered, Mr. Nwokedi. Unfortunately, we are powerless to influence the course of events...powerless to help you and your people. I ask you to forgive me...and my colleague, Mr. Donald. We believe in the justness of your cause.

JAMES DONALD: Prime Minister, I can no longer serve a government that is party to the eradication of a Christian people... People who never offended us... They were our natural allies. Your choice now is to defend these Christians by military intervention... or to appease fanatical Muslims hell bent on murdering them.

SIR HUGH: The Prime Minister must know that choosing to help Muslims destroy a Christian people will go down well with his pals in the European Union...They've been using Islam for decades now to erode and dismember what's left of Judeo-Christian civilization. Tell us, Prime Minister, does your ambition to be the voice of the globalist empire outweigh the moral necessity to save a Christian people? You'll have my resignation by day's end.

PRIME MINISTER

(enraged):   All right then, bloody do it! I'm sick of your sanctimonious recriminations! You deliberately avoid the consequences of prolonging this war by a military intervention! The Muslim junta will invite the Russians to send troops to oppose us, and we will be in a real war! Do you really think the public will want British lads to die? What will we gain? Nothing... Better to let the American deal go through...I have no good choices; can't you see that?

SIR HUGH: You have chosen your career over the lives of millions of innocent people.

(Silence)

ARCHBISHOP: I must protest, Sir Hugh! Your did not bear the responsibility for the enormous decisions the Prime Minister had to make. When forced to choose between two evils, you have to choose the lesser... the Prime Minister has chosen, and we must not judge him!

TONY NWOKEDI: We have to leave the final judgement to God and history, Archbishop. Contrary to your insistence that we must not judge, I beg to differ...we have to judge...as to what is good and what is evil.... God gave us that responsibility...When we decide not to judge evil as evil, we condemn ourselves to be destroyed by it. I refer, of course, to the Islam of General Musa and his fellow murderers in the junta.

ARCHBISHOP: You have no right to condemn Islam, Mr. Nwokedi! As the leader of the Anglican community, I condemn any form of intolerance and exclusion! That is unmitigated fascism! The people doing the killing in Benugu are not Muslim! They are criminals who have coerced a peaceful world religion.

TONY NWOKEDI: You know, Archbishop, we Christians of Benugu may be decimated, but those who survive will have their faith... You now have just the trappings... The ceremonies in Westminster, where you wear your long gorgeous robes, much like the Pharisees of Jesus' time. And you have your churches, most of them empty...which will soon be mosques... That is what a "Christian" church without Christ looks like...I will take my leave now...Thank you, Sir Hugh Mr. Donald. May God help us all?

(He walks out. Silence)

JAMES DONALD: His words have wounded me, Prime Minister... Apparently, I am still vulnerable to the truth.

SIR HUGH: His words have made me feel deeply ashamed. Our betrayal of a Christian people reminds me of another betrayal: when we abandoned Czechoslovakia to a monstrous evil...

(He looks atn the Prime Minister)

We had Churchill then, who defied his party and stood alone-to voice and defend the truth. We cannot expect that from you.

(The Prime Minister laughs rather hysterically)

PRIME MINISTER: The "truth?" Well, Sir Hugh, the truth is an elusive many-aspected thing, isn't it? Look, I know that Mr. Nwokedi must be inconsolable... I mean, who wouldn't be? But genocides happen... They've happened throughout history... But do we dwell on them? Six million Jews exterminated by Hitler, ten million Christians, Poles, Slavs, Gypsies, homosexuals...the physically and mentally disabled...You can't dwell on these abominations because they will destroy you. We have to come to terms with the horror of the human condition...And I am not responsible for creating it!

SIR HUGH: May I remind you, Sir, that we did not "come to terms" with it. We opposed it with our lives!

(He stands)

I will have my resignation delivered to your office this evening. Mr. Donald, shall we?

JAMES DONALD: Of course, Sir. I know you'll rise to glory and fame in the European Union, Prime Minister...you've shown me that you belong there.

(The two men leave. Silence. The archbishop fiddles nervously, and the Prime Minister stares vacantly at the door.)

PRIME MINISTER: You know Felicity, I stand condemned of a crime I didn't commit. I refuse to take the blame as the sole perpetrator of a genocide! Fate has not been kind to me, and history...yes, history will be brutal. I didn't make the rules of this vicious and ugly game I made my lifework... Looking at the big picture...I'm just a minor player in this unavoidable disaster.

(He looks at her and forces a smile)

And now I have to live with the pall of condemnation hanging over me for the rest of my life.

ARCHBISHOP: You mustn't judge yourself, Harry. We sin only when we clearly intend to. You never intended this horrid slaughter to happen. When we're thrown into a maelstrom of malevolence, we no longer have control...Sometimes, my dear friend, life sins against us by putting us in impossible situations. We are not then fully responsible for our actions, and that's why I never judge others. You must carry on, Harry...there's so much good you can do.

(Silence)

PRIME MINISTER: Well, you're right, Felicity. We have to move on, don't we? As Machiavelli said, a wise man never says no to the inevitable but always finds in it something he can use to his advantage. The war in Bengara will end soon, and I will get credit from the people who really matter... My colleagues in the European Union will certainly welcome a Muslim victory! Any erosion of Christianity fits in with their universal agenda. The Americans will applaud my decision not to intervene, and the British people will be happy that our lads weren't killed in an unwinnable war. Yes, Felicity, there's always a bright side to everything.

ARCHBISHOP: Of course, there is, Harry! You're a good man, and I'm proud of your many achievements...God has wonderful plans for you, so stay the course. You'll always have detractors, I mean, don't we all? But I will always be one of your most ardent supporters!

PRIME MINISTER: Thank you, Felicity. Your support and confidence mean a great deal to me.

ARCHBISHOP: Of course, I do expect something in return...

PRIME MINISTER: Of course...anything.

ARCHBISHOP: I want you to be the main speaker at the symposium I will soon be having on Islam... The theme is: "Islam, Illuminating Britain and the World." Will you, do it?

PRIME MINISTER: Anything that promotes diversity and inclusion has my unreserved support. It will be an honor, Archbishop!

(She gets up and embraces him)

ARCHBISHOP: Thank you, thank you, Harry. With a man like you   as our Prime Minister we can evolve into the nation we were meant to be...a rainbow of uncritical tolerance, open to the nonconformist and the alien, welcoming of the eccentric and unorthodox...We will finally be the Great Britain we've longed for...the New Jerusalem!

THE END

In 1948, the United Nations General Assembly agreed on the following definition of genocide:

"Acts committed with the intent to destroy, in whole or in part, a national, ethnical, racial, or religious group."

By this definition, Biafra was subjected to genocide by mass starvation and slaughter by a vastly superior military force between 1967 and 1970.

Disclaimer:

CALL IT GENOCIDE, *" a stage play by Eric Martin, is a fictional work. The characters, events, and settings portrayed are products of the author's imagination or are used fictitiously. Any resemblance to actual persons, living or deceased, events, or locales is entirely coincidental.*

www.ingramcontent.com/pod-product-compliance
Lightning Source LLC
Chambersburg PA
CBHW061744050726
47598CB00002B/582